FRIEND OR FOE

The Whole Truth about Animals That People Love to Hate

WRITTEN BY *ETTA KANER*

ILLUSTRATED BY *DAVID ANDERSON*

OWLKIDS BOOKS

For Stacey, with appreciation—E.K.

*To Catherine and our sons, John, Nicholas, and William,
for all your help and support—D.A.*

Text © 2015 Etta Kaner
Illustrations © 2015 David Anderson

Owlkids Books acknowledges the financial support of the Canada Council for the Arts, the Ontario Arts Council, the Government of Canada through the Canada Book Fund (CBF) and the Government of Ontario through the Ontario Media Development Corporation's Book Initiative for our publishing activities.

Published in Canada by
Owlkids Books Inc.
10 Lower Spadina Avenue
Toronto, ON M5V 2Z2

Published in the United States by
Owlkids Books Inc.
1700 Fourth Street
Berkeley, CA 94710

Library and Archives Canada Cataloguing in Publication

Kaner, Etta, author
     Friend or foe : the truth about animals people love to hate / written by Etta Kaner ; illustrated by David Anderson.

ISBN 978-1-77147-064-3 (bound)

     1. Animal diversity--Juvenile literature. 2. Animal ecology-- Juvenile literature. 3. Animal behavior--Juvenile literature.   I. Anderson, David, 1952 June 7-, illustrator II. Title.

QL49.K364 2015   j590.1'2   C2014-908456-0

Library of Congress Control Number: 2015900223

Edited by: Jennifer Stokes and John Crossingham
Designed by: Alisa Baldwin
Cover photo (vintage texture old paper): © Denys Kuralev, Dreamstime
Interior photo (old paper texture): © Spaxia, Dreamstime

Manufactured in Shenzhen, Guangdong, China, in June 2018, by WKT Co. Ltd.
Job #18CB0980

B   C   D   E   F   G

OWL kids Publisher of Chirp, Chickadee and OWL
www.owlkidsbooks.com

Contents

Introduction

Imagine this: You're playing a video game when a spider drops onto your screen. "Aah!" you scream as you fling your device across the room.

"What's the big deal?" asks your sister. "Spiders are awesome. Have you ever watched a spider spin a web? Do you know that spiders can…"

You can't believe it. Your sister actually loves spiders! Then you realize that even though many people are afraid of snakes, you think they are pretty cool.

When you think about it, people have different points of view about lots of animals. Take bees, for instance:

Bees can give you a NASTY STING, which may cause a serious ALLERGIC REACTION in some people.

Bees produce that HEAVENLY HONEY you slather on your pancakes and waffles.

And what about rats, mosquitoes, bats, cockroaches, leeches, and vultures? How do you feel about these animals? You'll get a chance to decide when you check out these and other animals explored in the next few pages.

On the one hand, you'll find arguments trying to convince you that these animals are disgusting, mean, dangerous, sneaky, or smelly.

On the other hand, you'll hear about how these very same animals are smart, helpful to humans and the environment, and an inspiration to scientists.

Though each side is telling the truth, both are trying to persuade you to agree with a certain point of view. Which side will you take?

Find out how you *really* feel about animals that people love to hate. Are they friend or foe?

OH, RATS!
PUBLIC ENEMY #1

GNASTY GNAWERS

See those sharp front teeth? Rats cause millions of dollars' worth of damage. They start house fires by gnawing on electrical wires. They eat harvested food and damage sugarcane and rice crops. Experts say that rats eat or destroy between one-fifth and one-third of the world's human food supply!

"Hey! A guy's gotta eat, doesn't he?"

DIRTY RAT. RAT FINK. PACK RAT.

No wonder people use these terms as insults. These buck-toothed rodents with their beady eyes and naked tails are considered to be the most destructive mammal on earth—other than humans, that is!

BEWARE THE RATS!

Ever heard of the bubonic plague, the disease that killed millions of people in many parts of the world? Whose fault was it? Rats (well, indirectly). People got the plague from rat fleas. The rat flea loved rat blood. When a plague-infected flea sucked a rat's blood, it injected the disease into the rat. When the rat died, its fleas looked for another meal ticket: people!

These nasty nibblers have also overrun small islands and destroyed many species of wildlife, including small ground birds and seabirds, small mammals, and reptiles, as well as seeds and plants. How? By hitching a ride on a ship and having *lots* of babies (a single pair of rats can produce 15,000 in just one year). As newcomers to an island, rats have no natural predators and local wildlife has no natural defenses.

CROOKS AND CRIMINALS

As if that's not bad enough, thanks to rats, 18 bird species (including species of flightless teal, snipe, and parakeet) are now extinct, and 40 more are on the endangered list. How is this possible? Bird eggs are number one on rats' shopping lists.

Have coins, keys, or jewelry gone missing from your home? A rat might be the thief. Rats love to hoard shiny objects in their nests. And watch out for that missing paper money, too. Rats in Abu Dhabi once ate 2 million dollars of cash stored in a sheikh's closet.

But, on the other hand...

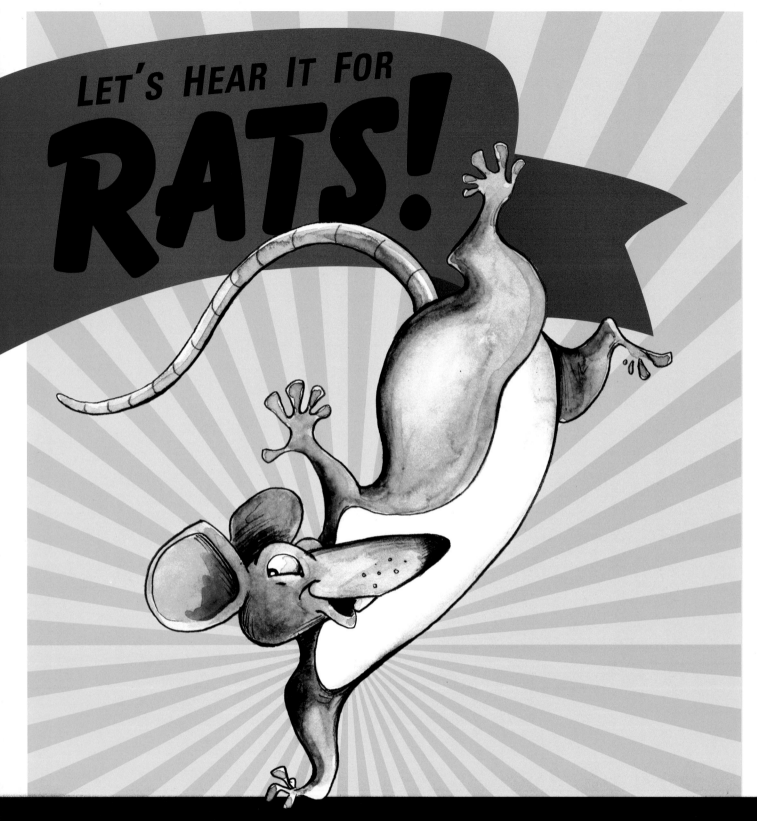

LET'S HEAR IT FOR **RATS!**

TEETH OF STEEL. ABLE TO **DODGE** SPEEDING CARS. **LEAPS** FROM GREAT HEIGHTS IN A SINGLE BOUND. **LOOK! IT'S SUPER RAT!** ACTUALLY, THAT WOULD BE **ANY** RAT.

Tiny gymnasts

Rats can scurry along telephone wires, scale brick walls, tread water for hours, squeeze through holes the size of a quarter, and land on their feet after falling five stories!

Rats aren't just agile acrobats. They're brainy, too. An English farmer once watched two rats stealing a chicken egg. One rat lay on its back holding the egg in its paws. The second rat slowly dragged the first one by its tail across the ground to the rat hole!

What big teeth you have!

It's true that rats are always chewing. But it just comes naturally to them. Rats must chew on hard objects to grind down teeth that keep growing throughout their lives. Chewing through plastic, rubber, wood, iron, lead, and even concrete is a no-strainer for their incredible chompers.

Those teeth come in handy for grooming, too. Rats are really picky about keeping clean and spend half their waking hours licking and nibbling their fur. How much time do you spend washing?

Cute, cuddly, and caring

Rats love to cuddle when they snooze. They nuzzle and groom each other. When rats are hurt or sick, family members look after them. They bring them food, free them from traps, and lead those that are blind with their tails.

Lifesavers

In parts of Africa, African giant pouched rats save the lives of millions of people with their supersensitive noses. Some are trained to detect a deadly disease called tuberculosis by sniffing people's saliva. Others sniff out dangerous buried land mines left over from wars. No wonder these amazing rats are called heroes!

"I'm posing for the cameras. Tourists at the Karni Mata temple in India think that sighting a white rat will bring them good luck."

"What are you doing?"

So, what do YOU think? Is a rat friend OR foe?

9

COCKROACHES— GET RID OF THEM!

WHERE ARE THEIR MANNERS?

Cockroaches feed on just about anything—sugar, bread, paper, soap, glue, leather, and yes, even the sweat in your armpits and the moisture in your nostrils. And their table manners? Dis-gusting. They poop on their food and vomit some of it as they eat. After stepping in this germy gunk, cockroaches move on to contaminate other surfaces with their soiled feet.

Cockroaches are cannibals—that means they sometimes eat each other. Nymphs (the young) will eat other nymphs, and mothers often eat their own eggs...even when other food is available. Definitely not the caring type of bug.

ACH-EWW!

Imagine living with a runny nose, a skin rash, or breathing trouble. That's what it's like for millions of people who suffer from allergies or allergic asthma caused by—what else?—cockroaches. These conditions are reactions to cockroach poop, shed skin, and odor.

CREEPY CRAWLERS

It's the middle of the night. You turn on the light to get a drink. What are those spots on the kitchen counter? Aah! Cockroaches! Your stomach does a double flip as those hard shiny bodies with their long, waving antennae skitter across the floor. It's enough to creep anyone out. Take a look…

DUCK! FLYING COCKROACHES OVERHEAD!

Have you ever been dive-bombed by flying cockroaches? That's what people living in places like Hawaii feel they're experiencing. While many cockroaches are strong fliers, they're lousy navigators. They often bump into people and things that are in their way. Even though these crashes are accidental, they're still gross.

Asian cockroaches are just as creepy. They'll follow you around in your home. These cockroaches love bright light. When you move from one room to another, turning on the lights, they'll fly after you. And don't let the name fool you—Asian cockroaches live in the southern United States as well as in Southeast Asia.

HOLD YOUR NOSE!

Cockroaches stink—especially noticeable when there's a large bunch of them. Some people say the smell is like bitter almond. This smell comes from a combination of their poop, saliva, and waxy skin.

But, on the other hand…

11

COOL COCKROACHES—
Get One Now!

Have you been bugging your parents for a pet, and they're still saying no? ***How about a cockroach?*** Really! It's quiet. It will eat almost anything, and you don't have to walk it. Surprised? What's more, cockroaches are actually helpful to humans and ecosystems.

Roaches to the rescue!

Scientists think Madagascar hissing cockroaches are ideal for finding people trapped in collapsed buildings with hard-to-reach spaces. These cockroaches can withstand extreme temperatures, get through small cracks, are great climbers, and can go with little or no food for weeks. Carrying electronic backpacks, these cockroaches could become the search-and-rescue animals of the future!

Having a snack attack?

Try a cockroach! Cockroaches are low in fat and high in protein. That makes them very healthy to eat. They are also easy to raise. It takes much less feed, land, and water to raise a pound of cockroach meat than it does to raise a pound of beef. Some scientists believe cockroaches can help solve world hunger—and help the environment at the same time!

And next time you feel sick, think cockroach. In some parts of the world, people use ground-up dried cockroaches to help heal earaches, stomachaches, broken bones, cuts, bruises, burns, sore throats, and insect stings.

Friends of the environment

It's not fair. Although all cockroaches get a bad rap, only four species actually invade our homes. Most of the other 5,000 cockroach species live in the wild and actually help our environment. How?

Cockroaches are like mini-composters. They spend a lot of time cleaning up the forest floor by devouring dead plants and animals. Their poop enriches the soil. Cockroaches also munch on mosquitoes and other insects. Thanks to cockroaches, there are fewer insects to bug you!

The already endangered red-cockaded woodpecker depends on cockroaches for half of its diet. Without cockroaches, this animal could be threatened with extinction. Cockroaches also make a great snack for other birds, as well as for lizards, frogs, scorpions, army ants, and monkeys.

"If you don't mind, I'd rather NOT be attacked for a snack."

So, what do YOU think? Is a cockroach friend OR foe?

SNAKES: SILENT AND DEADLY

DANGER! SNAKES ALIVE!

Every year, at least 20,000 people die worldwide from venomous snakebites. Most of these people live in Asia and Africa. Depending on the snake, its poison causes internal bleeding, paralysis, and other nasty reactions.

You don't have to be bitten by a snake to be affected by its venom. Some cobras spray venom out of their fangs and can hit a target 6 ft. (1.8 m) away. The venom can cause terrible pain and temporary blindness if it hits your eyes.

DON'T SNAKE UP ON ME LIKE THAT!

Snakes are sneaky. Most snakes lie in wait, camouflaged and motionless, until a tasty morsel passes by. Then they lunge out and grab their prey. Some snakes even wiggle their brightly colored tails as a lure when they spot a possible meal. When the prey stops to investigate, the snake strikes and the animal is *hiss*story.

NOT THE WHOLE THING!

Watching a snake eat can turn your stomach. Snakes swallow their prey whole, headfirst. A snake's jaws can open so wide that the snake can swallow an animal three times larger than its own head. That's like a human swallowing a basketball whole!

Have you ever noticed how snakes seem to sneak up on you? Their cold eyes hold you in their grip as if they're hypnotizing you. Their forked tongues check you out before they plunge their venomous fangs into your skin.

WATCH OUT!
SQUEEZERS AT WORK

Thinking of getting a boa or a python for a pet? Think again. These constrictors are dangerous! If they coil their powerful muscular bodies around you, it's game over. You're squeezed so tightly that you can't breathe or your blood stops flowing to your heart. It takes less than a minute for one of these snakes to squeeze a goat to death.

But, on the other hand...

SNAKES ARE SUPER!

LET'S GET ONE THING STRAIGHT: not all snakes are venomous! In fact, 80 percent of snakes are **NOT DANGEROUS** to humans. So, the next time you meet a snake, think about its beautiful skin patterns and how elegantly it glides across the ground.

Learning from snakes

Inspired by the shape of real snakes, Dr. Howie Choset, a scientist, invented Robo-Snake, a robot that slithers like a live snake. Robo-Snakes come in different sizes. Tiny snakebots with mini-cameras, scissors, and forceps help surgeons operate on human hearts and other diseased organs. Larger snakebots are used to get into hard-to-reach places for search-and-rescue work, to inspect radioactive areas of nuclear power plants, and even to explore archaeological ruins.

Other scientists are studying how the pits of pit vipers work. Pits are two tiny holes, one on each side of the face, with thousands of special cells that detect heat. These heat-sensitive cells allow pit vipers to zero in on prey in the dark. Scientists hope to use this knowledge to create devices that will find tumors in humans. Researchers are also using the pit viper's venom to create drugs to treat heart disease, high blood pressure, and cancer.

We love snakes!

Popular item on a restaurant menu in China? You got it! Snake. You'll find cobra soup, deep-fried snake meatballs, smoked snake, and leopard snake hot pot. The Chinese believe that eating snake helps cure rheumatism, poor eyesight, and bad skin. And the taste? Deeelicious! A lot like chicken.

What if snakes disappeared? Would it really matter? Absolutely! Picture these news headlines: "Plants Devoured by Masses of Snails, Slugs, and Insects." "Harvested Grain Consumed by Hordes of Rats." "Birds of Prey and Mongooses Starving and Endangered." And last but not least, "Chefs in China Very Upset!" Whether as prey or predator, snakes are an important part of ecosystems around the world.

"I'm glad pie-thon isn't on the menu!"

So, what do YOU think? Is a snake friend OR foe?

LEECHES SUCK

OUT FOR BLOOD!

Imagine being bitten by 300 razor-sharp teeth all at once. That's what might happen when a bloodsucking leech latches onto your skin. Once its tiny teeth make a Y-shaped cut, the leech sucks your blood until it's full. That could take about a half hour or so.

"Hey, we're not all bloodsuckers. One-quarter of us are carnivores!"

INVASION OF THE LEECHES

Leeches live everywhere—on land, in freshwater, and in oceans throughout the world. Some bloodsucking leeches will eat only the blood of a specific animal, such as fish, sharks, or bats. One species is even more revolting: it lives and feeds in the anus of hippos.

STILL BLEEDING

Even if you've managed to scrape a leech off your skin, you're not done with that slimy critter. The wound that it created will continue to bleed for up to 10 hours. Why? A chemical that the leech injects to keep the blood flowing as it sucks continues to work long after dinner is done.

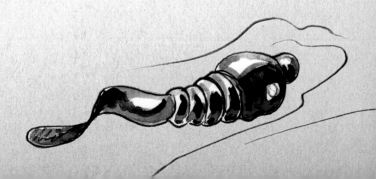

SLIMY VAMPIRES

Have you ever wondered why horror movies show leeches as the bad guys? Maybe it's because these creatures are basically mini-vampires. Once these slimy bloodsuckers take hold, they become very attached to you.

STAY OUT OF THE WATER

Is T. rex a thing of the past? Yes and no. T. rex—the *Tyrannobdella rex* leech—is alive and well and living in the Upper Amazon River. It uses its eight large teeth to bite into the mouth, nose, or throat of a human. And it doesn't drop off after feeding. It can remain attached for days or weeks, growing to the size of your forefinger. Warning: Don't swim in the Upper Amazon River!

Ever see a duck or swan vigorously shaking its head, scratching its bill, and sneezing? It could be trying to get rid of the leeches in its nasal passages, throat, or eyes. Leeches make it hard for these poor birds to breathe and can cause temporary blindness and even death in the young.

But, on the other hand...

LOVELY LEECHES

"Smile!"

Lake-savers

Leeches keep lakes healthy by eating rotting plants and animals found at the bottom. These mini–vacuum cleaners stop decaying debris from building up. This allows lake water to stay clean for living organisms.

Scientists use leeches to check the health of lakes—they call them the biomarkers of freshwater ecosystems. If leeches in a lake are few and far between, it might be because the water is too acidic for them to survive. This is a warning sign that fish and other animals would have a hard time living there, too. High five, leeches, on a job well done!

LIFESAVERS AND LAKE-SAVERS

Quick! Name two types of hospital workers. You probably said nurses and doctors. But what about leeches? They often work in hospitals, too. Leeches are amazing healers. And not just of humans. They also help keep our water ecosystems healthy.

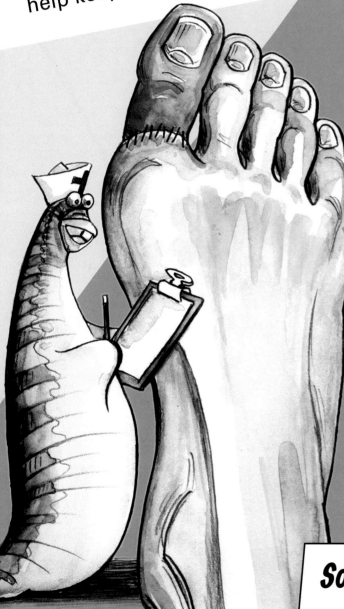

Lifesavers

If you're ever unlucky enough to lose a finger or toe in an accident, don't despair. Doctors can usually reattach it. The only problem is that after surgery, blood may build up in the reattached body part. This stops it from healing. Can anything help? Yes! Leeches to the rescue! Attach a leech to the wound, and as it feeds it injects hirudin, a chemical that stops blood clotting and keeps blood flowing. This gives tiny blood vessels a chance to heal.

Researchers have been studying hirudin to try to develop drugs to treat patients with heart disease. They have also been using leeches to relieve pain in people with osteoarthritis, a disease that causes stiffness and swelling of the joints. It's easy to understand why pain-free patients would become quite fond of these helpful leeches.

So, what do YOU think? Is a leech *friend* OR *foe?*

BATS— CREATURES OF THE DARK

Bats: with their leaflike noses, giant ears, and pointy teeth, they sure aren't a pretty sight. But much worse, bats often spread disease and hang out in spooky places where you might not want to be.

I've come to drink YOUR BLOOD!

See those teeth? They're as sharp as a knife blade. The common vampire bat uses them to cut into the skin of a sleeping animal so that it can lap up its blood. As if that's not bad enough, this bat urinates while dining.

How much blood does a vampire bat drink? About 2 tbsp. (30 mL) each night. That's not much blood for a cow to lose, right? The problem is that if a bat is infected with rabies, it passes this horrible disease on to the cow. Cattle dying from rabies is a major problem for farmers (and cows) in Central and South America.

Watch where YOU'RE STEPPING!

Enter any bat cave and you'll step in globs of guano. Guano is bat poop, which piles up on the floor of a cave or any other place where bats roost. Guano in a crowded cave could be as high as a seven-story building! In warmer parts of the world, guano contains histoplasmosis, a fungus disease that can make people very sick.

Don't blame the BED BUGS

Feeling itchy? Don't be too quick to blame bed bugs. It might be bat mites that are making you scratch. Bat mites normally feed on bat blood. But if you've had a recent visit from a bat, bat mite hitchhikers may have stayed behind and are now looking for a new dining experience: you!

But, on the other hand...

GO TO BAT FOR BATS!

So all bats are ugly, you say? *Come on. You've got to admit that the face of this fruit bat is sooo loveable. Just look at those appealing eyes and those perky ears. It looks like a small dog with wings. But bats shouldn't be judged by appearance alone. Talk to farmers and scientists, and they'll tell you how valuable bats are.*

Echo echo echo…

How do bats find insects in the dark? They use echolocation. Echolocation is a way of locating an object by sending out sound waves that echo or bounce back from it to the sender (the bat). The echoes bats hear tell them the size, shape, texture, and location of insects. Scientists studying this amazing ability have invented devices that can map ocean floors, find schools of fish, detect disease in human bodies, and help blind people get around.

Thank you, bats

But not all bats echolocate. Bats that eat fruit or drink nectar use their sight and keen sense of smell to find food. Thanks to these bats, tropical rain forests are able to regenerate. How? Seeds dropped by fruit-eating bats as they eat or poop grow into new plants. And the pollen powder that nectar-drinking bats carry on their fur from one flower to another forms seeds so new fruit grows. The next time you eat a mango or date or fig, think of the bats that had a hand…er, seed, in growing it.

Farmers' friends

Farmers are ecstatic about bats, especially their guano. They use it to fertilize their fruit and vegetable crops. The natural chemicals in guano grow healthy plants with strong roots and stems. Farmers also applaud bats for eating the many insect pests that ruin their crops.

That's my mom

Bats are devoted mothers. When a mother bat returns to the roost to nurse her pup, she fights off hundreds of other pups that are trying to steal her milk. She doesn't stop until she finds her young one, having thoroughly sniffed its body before nursing to make sure it's hers.

"These kids are driving me batty."

So, what do YOU think? Is a bat friend OR foe?

AAH! SHARKS!

THE BETTER TO EAT YOU WITH, MY DEAR

Every year around the world, sharks attack between 70 and 100 human swimmers. It's true that not many people die from these attacks. But just one chomp from those steak-knife-like teeth can do a lot of damage.

Many sharks like an easy meal. Some pick on prey that is ill, injured, or immature—animals that won't get away in a chase. Others bite large chunks out of dead whales and seals as they float down to the seabed. Tiger sharks eat whatever they find, including paint cans, life jackets, wire, clothing, dogs, and people.

STOMACH UPSET

How does a shark get rid of hard-to-digest bones and shells? It turns its stomach inside out and vomits it right out of its mouth! Once the indigestible pieces are dumped into the water, the shark swallows its stomach. Not a pretty sight.

MEAN MOUTHS

Babies are sweet and innocent, right? Not unborn sand tiger sharks. The largest baby or pup in the womb devours all of its brothers and sisters. When the fully grown pup emerges, it makes a fast getaway in case it becomes its mother's next meal.

The cookiecutter shark sneaks up on tuna, dolphins, and whales and latches on to their skin with its sucker-like mouth. Its blade-like teeth act like an ice cream scoop to dig out a chunk of flesh. Ouch! The painful wound that it leaves can easily become infected.

MONSTERS OF THE DEEP

What could be more terrifying than seeing a shark fin heading right toward you? Will the shark's saw-like teeth rip you to shreds? Or will you live to tell the tale? Don't wait to find out. Get out of the water, fast!

But, on the other hand...

SHARKS— WONDERS OF

"Next!"

Oops! I made a mistake

Okay. Sometimes sharks do attack people. But it's often a case of mistaken identity. Paddling surfboarders, when seen from below, look like the seals and sea turtles that sharks eat. Once a shark realizes that the person in its jaws is not a blubbery animal, it spits him or her out.

All in a mouth's work

What do whale sharks and basking sharks, the largest fish in the sea, eat? Plankton—microscopic plants and animals. As the shark slowly swims along, thousands of gallons of water enter its cavernous mouth and exit through its gills. A fine mesh strains out the plankton, which moves to the back of the mouth. Then it's—gulp!—down the hatch.

Forget *Jaws*. You're too smart to believe all that hype. Sharks aren't interested in eating people. They'd rather eat a plump seal than a bony human any day. But eating isn't all they do. Many protect the little guy in the sea.

THE SEA

"Three thousand teeth and I'm still not done. Next time I'll (tooth) pick a smaller shark."

Not everything that enters a shark's mouth is food. Finger-sized fish called wrasse nibble gunk off a shark's teeth with no danger of being eaten. These little dentists also clean lice and other parasites off the shark's gills and body.

Other cleaner fish called remora hitch rides by attaching themselves to sharks with the sucker-like fin they have on their heads. Not only do they get a free ride and free food, but they're also protected from larger fish that wouldn't dare come near a shark.

Swim like a shark

Are you into competitive swimming? If so, you might want to wear the kind of swimsuit that Olympic swimmers have worn. It was inspired by sharks!

A shark's skin is covered with tiny grooved scales. The grooves are lined up to form channels along which water flows down the shark's body. This reduces the resistance of the water, making the shark a superfast swimmer.

So, what do YOU think? Is a shark **friend OR foe?**

SPIDERS:

SNEAKY spiders

Many spiders are tricky hunters. Lynx spiders sneak up and pounce on their prey like a cat. Crab spiders wait camouflaged in flowers for bees and butterflies to come within easy reach. Spiders that mimic ants have no problem sneaking into an ant nest to gobble up the larvae.

Some spiders are thieves. Instead of capturing their own prey, they sneak into a web and snatch its owner's catch. They even have the nerve to cut out sections of the web and roll it up to eat. Sometimes, webs get so infested with these intruders that the host is forced to move.

BAD date

Male spiders looking for a mate might not survive the first date. Since males are usually much smaller than females, they can easily be mistaken for prey. Males try all sorts of tricks to avoid being eaten. Some bring a silk-wrapped insect as a gift. Others dance or sing for the female. In spite of these efforts, males often become meals.

30

Scary, Sneaky, and Spooky

Remember those cute spider songs you sang in kindergarten? Don't kid yourself. Spiders are not cute! Spiders have bizarre faces with multiple eyes and venomous fangs, leave messy webs in your home, and drop down beside you when you're eating your curds and whey. Yikes!

Oh, the PAIN!

If you think being bitten by a rattlesnake is your worst nightmare, think again. A black widow spider's venom is 15 times more potent than a rattlesnake's. There is an antivenin that can help you recover from this nasty bite, but the pain of the bite is a 10 out of 10. So be careful!

Instant SOUP

Ever see an insect that doesn't move when you approach it? It might be because a spider got to it first. A spider uses venom to paralyze prey and turn its insides to mush. The spider sucks its victim dry, leaving behind a hollow body. What a way to go.

But, on the other hand...

SPIDERS ARE SPECTACULAR!

World Wide Web

Did you know that some spider silk is five times stronger than the same amount of steel? Not only is it superstrong, it's also stretchy, lightweight, and waterproof. That's why scientists have been trying to mimic spider silk for years. Just imagine what it could be used for! Medical scientists now have a silklike material that repairs deep cuts, nerves, and joints in humans. The next time you need stitches, the doctor might be using thread inspired by spider silk!

Other scientists are studying the nature of spider silk in the hopes of developing bulletproof clothing, artificial skin for burn victims, safer vehicle air bags, and adhesives that can be used under water. Biodegradable water bottles, bridge cables, and unrippable paper are also on the list of future inventions inspired by spider silk.

Shooting webs, flinging lassos, wearing master disguises, scaling sheer walls, flying through the air...these are the feats of superheroes, right? And the real superheroes are spiders. They do all this and more!

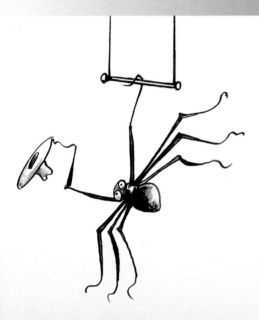

The terminator!

Irritated by earwigs, flies, or cockroaches in your home? Just invite a few spiders to dinner, and they'll take care of them. Spiders also eat the many pests that damage farmers' crops. People in East Africa are especially grateful for a jumping spider called "the mosquito terminator." It devours the kind of mosquito that transmits malaria to humans. Maybe this spider is the solution to getting rid of this deadly disease!

It's for the birds

Every year, about 100 million birds die from flying into glass windows. Glass is invisible to birds. But spider webs aren't. They reflect ultraviolet light, which birds can see. This gave researchers an idea. They created glass with a pattern of lines that reflect ultraviolet light. Since this makes windows look like a solid barrier to birds, they avoid them.

So, what do YOU think? Is a spider friend OR foe?

What do "The Three Little Pigs" and "Little Red Riding Hood" have in common? The Big Bad Wolf. In these stories and many others, the wolf is depicted as frightening, dangerous, and grandmother-devouring. Why? Because that's what they're really like (except for the devouring grandmothers part).

"Hey! Bad weather kills more cattle and sheep than wolves do."

THE BIG

CHOMP!

Wolves are not dainty eaters. They tear off large chunks of meat from their victim and wolf them down. Their sharp teeth and strong jaws easily chew through bones and hides. A wolf can scarf down as much as 20 lb. (9 kg) of meat in one sitting. That's like you eating 64 large hamburgers for supper!

Wolves may not eat grandmothers, but they have been known to attack children. This happens in rural areas of Europe and Asia, especially India, where children are left alone to look after livestock. Wolves see them as easy prey.

PUBLIC ENEMY #1!

That's how many ranchers who raise cattle and sheep see wolves. Farmers aren't fans of wolves either. In addition to killing cows and sheep, wolves kill poultry, small farm animals, and even pets if they're available.

34

Bad Wolf

Okay. A wolf's gotta eat. But who does it pick on? Animals that are young, sick, old, or weak. This means wolf packs can sometimes catch large animals, like elk, moose, and deer, without using a lot of energy.

Wolves are BULLIES

Every wolf pack has one wolf that's the underwolf, er…underdog. Other members of the pack threaten him or beat up on him, and he's the last one to get to feed at a kill. Sometimes this wolf gets so fed up with his mistreatment that he leaves the pack.

But, on the other hand...

WOLVES ARE WONDERFUL!

Playtime

Tag, mock fighting, hide-and-seek, toss and catch—all are games that wolves love to play. Pups play them all the time. Adult wolves play after sharing a good meal or just before starting out on a group hunt. Play builds trust among pack members. This is especially important since wolves use teamwork to catch large prey.

All in the family

Pack members look out for one another. If a mother is out hunting, a babysitter cares for her pups. When a pack returns from a hunt, its members share their meal with wolves that were too sick, too young, or too old to be part of the hunt. How? By vomiting partly digested food. A great way to bring home the groceries!

When wolves aren't playing, hunting, sleeping, or eating, they spend their time howling. Wolf howls avoid fights between packs by saying, "This is our territory. Stay away." Within a pack, howling helps pack members keep track of each other when they're apart.

You don't have to be a wolf to hear howling. Hundreds of tourists visit parks during the summer for wolf-howl nights. Staff naturalists imitate howls, hoping that wolves will answer them. And they often do!

"Howl's it going?"

Wolves are the ancestors of your precious pooch. Just like your dog, wolves are loyal to their family or pack. What's more, wolves are smart, courageous, loving, and playful. Sound familiar?

Save our wolves, save our environment

What happens when wolves are eliminated from an area? Without wolves to keep their numbers down, elk take over the land. They nibble trees and plants down to the bare ground. That's what happened in Yellowstone National Park, in the United States.

When wolves were allowed to return, incredible changes took place. To avoid the wolves, elk stayed away from streams. Aspen, cottonwood, and willow trees grew back. Once these trees grew, beavers reappeared to build dams, which created wetlands. The wetlands became a home for frogs, fish, ducks, muskrats, and otters. Wildflowers on the banks attracted insects, which brought birds that nested in the trees. And most amazing of all, the water quality of streams improved because the trees stopped soil from eroding into them. Where would nature be without wolves!

So, what do YOU think? Is a wolf **friend OR foe?**

Which do you think is the most dangerous animal in the world—the lion, polar bear, rattlesnake, crocodile, rhino… or mosquito? If you chose the mosquito, you are right. Really! **It may be small, but its bite can be deadly.**

Mosquitoes kill millions of people every year in some parts of the world. How? By infecting them with life-threatening diseases such as malaria, yellow fever, dengue fever, and West Nile virus. As these tiny vampires suck up blood, they inject spit that may contain a fatal disease.

Malaria kills birds, too—especially those that live on islands. And guess who the culprit is. Mosquitoes, of course. These bloodsuckers have caused 10 species of Hawaiian birds to become extinct, with several more on their way.

MOSQUITOES

RUN FOR YOUR LIVES!

Ever wonder why migrating caribou run so quickly across the tundra? They're trying to escape the clouds of mosquitoes that are driving them crazy. As well as covering the caribous' bodies, mosquitoes get into their mouths and nostrils. Caribou can suffocate from breathing in so many mosquitoes.

LOVE SONGS

A female mosquito's hum sounds like a love song to male mosquitoes. But male mosquitoes can be attracted to other humming things, too—like the hum of a power station. Once, a station in Canada kept breaking down—until engineers discovered that thousands of lovesick mosquitoes were gumming up the works.

I'M NOT A NEST!

Mosquitoes don't just leave behind an itch. If you lived in Central or South America, they might also leave the eggs of a botfly. A botfly glues its eggs to a mosquito's abdomen. As the mosquito feeds on your blood, the eggs hatch and their larvae burrow under your skin. Imagine larvae growing inside you! Yuck!

SMALL BUT DEADLY

"What's that awful sound?"

"It's those pesky mosquitoes whining and dining."

But, on the other hand...

It's not fair to paint all mosquitoes with the same blood, er…brush. **Not all species are bloodsuckers.** *Of the very few that are, the females have a blood meal only to lay their eggs. Besides, many animals and plants depend on mosquitoes, and scientists even learn from them!*

MARVELOUS
MOSQUITOES

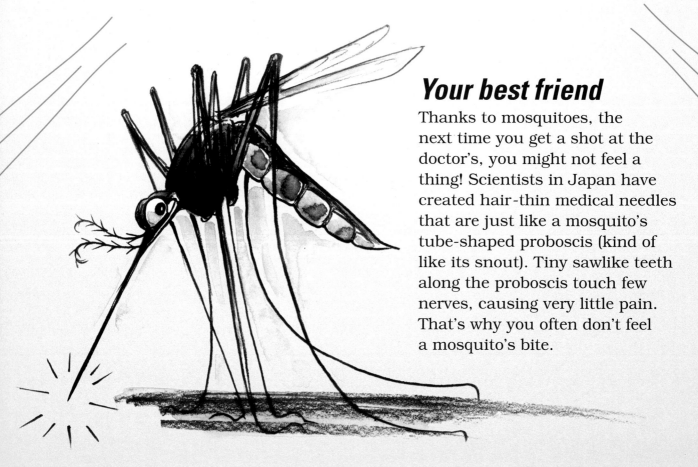

Your best friend

Thanks to mosquitoes, the next time you get a shot at the doctor's, you might not feel a thing! Scientists in Japan have created hair-thin medical needles that are just like a mosquito's tube-shaped proboscis (kind of like its snout). Tiny sawlike teeth along the proboscis touch few nerves, causing very little pain. That's why you often don't feel a mosquito's bite.

SLURP SLURP

How sweet it is!

If you were a mosquito, you would spend all day eating sweets. Both males and females satisfy their sweet tooth by drinking nectar from flowers. Mosquitoes also suck up juices from plants and fruit and feast on a sticky, sugary liquid called honeydew. No, this honeydew is not the melon. It's poop that's dropped by insects like aphids!

Spread it around

It's lucky for plants that mosquitoes like nectar. This is especially true for rare flowers such as Arctic orchids. They grow in a cold, barren climate, with few insects to pollinate them. But this doesn't bother mosquitoes. They fly from flower to flower gorging on nectar. At the same time, pollen powder sticks to their heads. When this pollen rubs off in the next flower, a seed starts to grow. Thanks to mosquitoes, Arctic orchids continue to survive.

Mosquitoes on the menu

Many birds, insects, salamanders, frogs, lizards, and spiders gobble up mosquitoes. And it's not just the adults that are popular. Hundreds of species of fish, like mosquitofish, depend on mosquito larvae for their diet. As well as being fish bait, mosquito larvae clean up water ecosystems by feeding on decaying leaves and matter. You could call them mini-recyclers!

So, what do YOU think? Is a mosquito *friend* OR *foe?*

41

HERE COME THE VULTURES!

Can you imagine anything weirder than this lappet-faced vulture with its wrinkly bald head and snakelike neck? If that's not bad enough, these smelly creatures spend much of their time cruising around looking for rotting dead animals to eat. How sickening is that?

Vile habits

To defend itself from danger, a turkey vulture vomits on its predator. Its vomit can spray as far as 6 ft. (1.8 m). Once the threat has passed, the vulture gulps down its vomit. No sense in wasting good food!

How does a vulture cool off on hot days? It poops on its legs. Since bird poop is mostly liquid, it evaporates, taking the heat with it. It's like you cooling off when your sweat evaporates—just a lot smellier.

Favorite vulture food? Carrion—the flesh of dead animals. Once larger vultures tear open a carcass with their strong beaks, turkey vultures and others dig right in. Getting bloody, smelly, gooey guts all over their heads and necks doesn't bother them one bit.

Where's the air freshener?

Vultures stink. And no wonder. The carrion they eat is often loaded with reeking, poisonous bacteria. As if that's not bad enough, they bring this rotting meat back to their nest to feed to their young. They vomit it right into their mouths. But startled young often spit up food, making the nest so smelly that vulture babies rarely become food for predators. Living in stink does have its advantages!

It's all mine!

Vultures don't share. They fight over carrion, even ripping pieces of meat out of each other's mouths. Larger species bully smaller vultures by chasing them away with open wings and jabbing beaks. Some vultures, like the king vulture, are so vicious that other scavengers leave when they arrive on the scene.

"What's that horrible smell?"

"There must be a vulture nearby."

But, on the other hand...

43

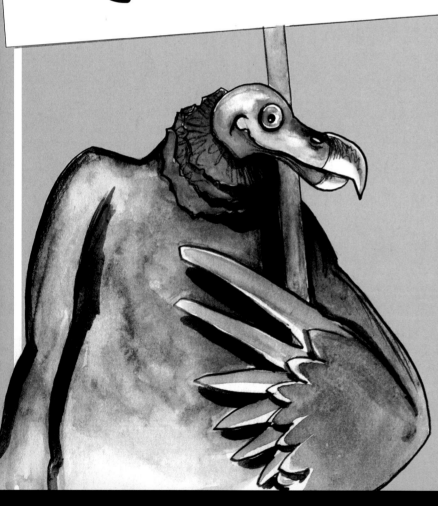

VULTURES DESERVE BETTER PRESS!

Eating leftovers

While most vultures eat meat, they usually don't kill it. Vultures eat animals that are already dead. These animals may have died from accidents or of old age, starvation, or deadly diseases, such as anthrax or hog cholera.

By eating diseased animals, vultures stop the disease from spreading to other animals, including you. What's amazing is that they never get an upset stomach. Once the diseased meat has passed through their digestive system, their poop is mostly bacteria-free!

You know that expression, "Never judge a book by its cover"? Just because vultures aren't cute and cuddly doesn't mean that they're not smart and helpful to your health and the environment. And one more thing: Not all vultures eat meat. One species is vegetarian!

Lunch is served…OVER THERE!

Hyenas, ravens, and vultures keep a close eye on a vulture in the air. When they see it descend, they make a beeline for the spot where the vulture touches down. There's a good chance that lunch is being served there.

Bird brains are SMART brains

An Egyptian vulture's favorite food is bird eggs—the bigger the better, like ostrich eggs. There's only one problem. Ostrich eggs have very tough shells. What does this clever bird do? It picks up a rock with its beak and throws it at the egg. It takes several tries to break the shell, but the yummy insides are worth the effort. (Ravens think so too when they eat the leftovers!)

Found it!

Vultures' food-finding talents—especially those of turkey vultures—help people. Turkey vultures use their supersensitive sniffers to locate carrion. Carrion smells like gas. When a gas company sees these birds circling over a spot, it's sure to investigate. The turkey vultures could very well be smelling gas leaking from underground pipes. Thanks to these vultures, the gas company is able to find and fix the leak, keeping us safe.

"I wish he'd hurry up and break open that egg."

"Egg-sactly! I'm raven-ous."

So, what do YOU think? Is a vulture *friend* OR *foe?*

45

Animals
ARE JUST
Doing Their Thing

I'll bet you had a hard time deciding whether some of the animals described in this book are friend or foe. That's probably because you realized that no animal is really bad or good. Animals just are what they are! Seeing them as friend or foe depends on the time and place, and a person's point of view.

Take rabbits, for instance. In North America, lots of people have rabbits as pets. But in Australia, rabbits are pests. That's because millions of rabbits have nibbled their way across Australia, destroying crops as well as the homes and food of other animals.

And what about wolves? In America in the early 1900s, many farmers complained that wolves were killing their livestock. Hunters said that wolves were competing with them for game. After a lot of pressure from both groups, the U.S. government hired people to get rid of tens of thousands of wolves. Sadly, it took decades for people to realize how important wolves actually are for keeping an ecosystem healthy.

But in the end, those rabbits and wolves that upset people are just doing what all animals do: they are trying to survive by eating food, having young, and staying away from predators.

So when you're upset with or scared by an animal, remember that it's just living its life. Chances are that if you could see the world as it does, you'd agree that it's neither friend nor foe: just an important part of nature.

Index

Sources

Beccaloni, Jan *Arachnids* Berkley, CA: University of California Press 2009

Berenbaum, May R. *Bugs in the System: Insects and their Impact on Human Affairs* Reading, MA: Addison-Wesley 1995

Berenbaum, May R. *The Earwig's Tail: a Modern Bestiary of Multi-legged Legends* Cambridge, MA: Harvard University Press 2009

Berenbaum, May R. *Ninety-nine Gnats, Nits and Nibblers* Urbana, IL: University of Illinois Press 1989

Bright, Michael *Sharks* Washington, DC: Smithsonian Institution Press 2002

Conniff, Richard *Rats! The Good, the Bad and the Ugly* New York, NY: Crown Publishers 2002

Copeland, Marion *Cockroach* London, UK: Reaktion 2003

Dalton, Stephen *Spiders: The Ultimate Predators* Richmond Hill, ON: Firefly Books 2008

Fenton, M. Brock *Bats* Markham, ON: Fitzhenry and Whiteside 2001

Fenton, M. Brock *The Bat: Wings in the Night Sky* Toronto, ON: Key Porter 1998

Gordon, David George *The Compleat Cockroach: A comprehensive guide to the most despised (and least understood) creature on earth* Berkley, CA: Ten Speed Press 1996

Gregory, Josh *From Bats to ... Radar* Ann Arbor, MI: Cherry Lake Pub. 2013

Harman, Jay *The Shark's Paintbrush: Biomimicry and how nature is inspiring innovation* Ashland, OR: White Cloud Press 2013

Hillyard, Paul *The Private Life of Spiders* Princeton, NJ: Princeton University Press 2008

Langton, Jerry *Rat: How the World's Most Notorious Rodent Clawed its Way to the Top* Toronto, ON: Key Porter Books 2006

Lee, Dora *Biomimicry: Inventions Inspired by Nature* Toronto, ON: Kids Can Press 2011

Kirk, Robert G. W. *Leech* London, UK: Reaktion 2012

Mara, Wil *From Sharks to... Swimsuits* Ann Arbor, MI: Cherry Lake Pub. 2013

Marrin, Albert *Oh Rats: the Story of Rats and People* New York, NY: Dutton Children's Books 2006

Marrin, Albert *Little Monsters: the Creatures That Live in Us and on Us* New York, NY: Dutton Children's Books 2011

Mattison, Christopher *The New Encyclopedia of Snakes* Princeton, NJ: Princeton University Press 2007

Ricciuti, Ed *The Snake Almanac: a Fully Illustrated Natural History of Snakes Worldwide* Guilford, CT: Lyons Press 2001

Steel, Rodney *Sharks of the World* New York, NY: Facts on File 2002